Millie's Tale

A play

Jean McConnell

Samuel French—London
New York-Toronto-Hollywood

Copyright © 2005 by Jean McConnell
All Rights Reserved

MILLIE'S TALE is fully protected under the copyright laws of the British Commonwealth, including Canada, the United States of America, and all other countries of the Copyright Union. All rights, including professional and amateur stage productions, recitation, lecturing, public reading, motion picture, radio broadcasting, television and the rights of translation into foreign languages are strictly reserved.

ISBN 978-0-573-02375-0

www.samuelfrench.co.uk
www.samuelfrench.com

FOR AMATEUR PRODUCTION ENQUIRIES

UNITED KINGDOM AND WORLD EXCLUDING NORTH AMERICA

plays@samuelfrench.co.uk
020 7255 4302/01

Each title is subject to availability from Samuel French, depending upon country of performance.

CAUTION: Professional and amateur producers are hereby warned that MILLIE'S TALE is subject to a licensing fee. Publication of this play does not imply availability for performance. Both amateurs and professionals considering a production are strongly advised to apply to the appropriate agent before starting rehearsals, advertising, or booking a theatre. A licensing fee must be paid whether the title is presented for charity or gain and whether or not admission is charged.

The professional rights in this play are controlled by Samuel French Ltd, 52 Fitzroy Street, London, W1T 5JR.

No one shall make any changes in this title for the purpose of production. No part of this book may be reproduced, stored in a retrieval system, or transmitted in any form, by any means, now known or yet to be invented, including mechanical, electronic, photocopying, recording, videotaping, or otherwise, without the prior written permission of the publisher. No one shall upload this title, or part of this title, to any social media websites.

The right of Jean McConnell to be identified as author of this work has been asserted in accordance with Section 77 of the Copyright, Designs and Patents Act 1988.

MILLIE'S TALE

First performed at the Oast Theatre, Tonbridge on 16th February 2005 with the following cast:

Eddie	Keith Rotchell
Lisa	Monica Dennington
Mrs Elms	Anne Cleverton
Belle Saunter	Janet Thompson
Herbie Saunter	Tony Holden
Sandra	Kate Bird

Directed by Jean McConnell
Designed and Stage Managed by Pamela Murphy

CHARACTERS

Eddie, careworker at Westways, ex-comedian; 50
Lisa, local newspaper journalist; 30
Mrs Elms, owner-manager of Westways; 50
Belle Saunter, English but for years in the USA; 60
Herbie Saunter, New Jersey American, Belle's husband; 60
Sandra, Australian; 40s

The action takes place in the main room of Westways Rest Home

Time — the present

AUTHOR'S NOTE

The refusal of the local Council to meet Millie's funeral costs, as detailed in Eddie's first speech, is based on a real-life case, as reported in the press at the time.

How to make and operate the champagne bottle containing the feather bouquet.

Take a bunch of coloured ostrich feathers about fourteen inches long. Secure together tightly at the base of the quills. Push the base of the quills into a slender cardboard tube and gently feed the feathers in to the tip. Take an empty champagne bottle. Aim the tube with the tips of the feathers at the neck of the bottle and gently ease the feathers down into the bottle until only the base quills protrude. Eddie shakes the bottle, holding the neck end with the base quills concealed in his hand. Then on cue he pulls the base and feathers out of the bottle and flourishes them. They will then spring into a bouquet.

Jean McConnell

Other plays by Jean McConnell
published by Samuel French Ltd:

Deckchairs I
Deckchairs II
Deckchairs III
A Lovesome Thing

With Miles Tripp:

Death is Catching

MILLIE'S TALE

The main room of Westways Rest Home

The place has an air of being in the middle of refurbishment. There is an entrance door leading to a front hall UR. *There are doors leading to Mrs Elm's office* UL *and to the kitchen* L. *There are three chairs: one set* UC, *one* L *and another* R. *There is a divan seat* C

Eddie enters from the hall. He is a careworker and long-term employee at the home. He was once a stand-up comic and still likes to clown around. He is wearing a strong apron and carrying a screwdriver. He moves DS

Eddie (*addressing the audience*) I tell you — it shocked me. And I take shocking. Mrs Elms blurted it out. I mean she wouldn't normally. Not that one. Normally a letter to the manager about an inmate of Westways Rest Home would be stashed away in the files. Very confidential. But we all thought a lot of old Millie. Millie had nothing. We all knew that. But I don't think Mrs Elms would have gone to the local authority except the home was going through one of its bad patches — the fire escape problem again. She was strapped. Pared the staff down to the core. Fired the core. Me. Then hauled me back. Mind you that was a regular event. Dutch Elm disease I called it. "Eddie, you're fired!" she'd shriek. And the old folk — my devoted public — would start snivelling. And she'd give in. We rubbed along. But trying to meet all the new regulations was murder. *En suite* rooms. Handrails every three inches. Ramps up. Ramps down. Ramps a go-go. Mrs Elms did everything they asked. Then they asked more. Then more. They'd been glad enough to dump Millie in Westways when it suited them. Reasonable, I reckon, to ask them to pay the funeral costs.

So, all right, they refused. But it was how they put it got to us. They said — and I quote — "Millie Budgen's body should be considered to be the 'industrial waste' of the home. Our Millie. Industrial waste!" Bloody industrial waste! (*He controls his anger*) I don't know who rang the local rag ... Well, all right, it was me. Anyway, this reporter showed up.

A doorbell rings

Eddie moves us *taking off his apron and exits into the hall. He enters showing Lisa into the room. She is a go-getting reporter, who strides in looking around with distaste*

Lisa Why do these places always smell so ghastly? If someone could invent something to counteract ammonia they'd make a fortune.
Eddie Well, the old folk are gone. It must be you.
Lisa If you need me to be helpful, watch your mouth.
Eddie You want this information or don't you?
Lisa We'll see. (*She sits down. She takes a tiny recorder, a notebook and pen out of her bag*) You fancy yourself as a whistleblower, Eddie. It is Eddie?
Eddie When I last looked.
Lisa This may not be a smart career move, Eddie.
Eddie Career? What's that? Oh I get it, you don't believe me.
Lisa Just testing.
Eddie Look sweetheart, I rang you in a bloody rage. But if you're not interested ...
Lisa No, it's a good story.
Eddie It's not a story!
Lisa I mean, it's of public interest. Would get them right here. (*She thumps her heart*)
Eddie Some daft sod in the council office ...
Lisa Insensitive, it seems. Unwise that's for sure.
Eddie As he'll find.
Lisa I must get a copy of that letter. Can you lay hands on one, Eddie?

Millie's Tale 3

Eddie (*shaking his head*) Strictly against all the rules, lady, and more than my job's worth. Here you are.

Eddie whips a letter out of his pocket and presents it

Lisa (*taking the letter*) Ta. (*She reads the letter*) God! Industrial waste.
Edde "Industrial waste"! Millie. You didn't know her.
Lisa So tell me.

Throughout the following Lisa takes the odd note in her notebook

Eddie She came here yonks ago. And just stayed. Did simple jobs.
Lisa You mean she was simple?
Eddie No way. More — sort of — dreamy. She'd had a baby. Way back. And then some sort of — breakdown. She was mostly OK but — you know — sometimes the light was off. It was in there but she didn't always switch it on. She laid the tables. Easy things. Never minded emptying the old girls' pots. Nor a bit of a ribbing. Liked a laugh. Best audience I ever had. Always got the point. I could have done with a row of Millies when I was in the business. Followed me round, helping.
Lisa And your function, Eddie? Handyman?
Eddie Careworker if you don't mind. And resident jester. Open the fridge door and I'll do my twenty minutes. (*Singing*) Make 'em laugh! (*Leaning in to Lisa; speaking*) There were two cannibals eating a clown. One said to the other, "Does this taste funny to you?" (*Singing*) Make 'em laugh! (*Speaking*) You know the sort of thing.
Lisa OK. But the old folk have left?
Eddie Yes. I emptied the house. As usual. No. Mrs E.'s transplanted them while we do the alterations. One whiff of DIY and the old dears are rolling up their sleeves. Not that Mrs E. discourages it. No. She sacked that layabout gardener and the old boys took over the veggie patch themselves. Loving it. But Mrs Elms is running herself ragged. If we can refurbish according to requirements — you know, five star hotel stuff — they'll all be back. We'll be a family again. Except for Millie. I'll miss her. She relied on me.

Everyone should have that. I relied on her relying on me. I'd fill up her forms ... Write her letters for her ...
Lisa Letters?
Eddie Oh, sending for offers and that. Cards for the old biddies' birthdays. And I'd write to the children's home for her. Way back they'd tried to get the baby released for adoption. But she'd have none of it. Always thought she'd get it back. 'Course it wasn't on. But she was pure gold. Gold. Not industrial waste!
Lisa What did Millie Budgen die of?
Eddie Cancer. Poor little bitch.
Lisa You said she had a baby.
Eddie Yes. It was put in this children's home up in the north. Not heard from them for years. Given up trying to get the release order signed, I suppose. Mrs Elms wrote to them once. But they said the child wasn't there any more.
Lisa Maybe they swung an adoption anyway. Would have been the best idea. To give the child a new life.
Eddie Millie always said she'd have the baby back one day. I couldn't make her understand it wasn't a baby any more. It had to be growing up. But she couldn't take it in. Used to nurse that old rag doll of hers. As if it was just taking her real baby's place — for the time being, like.
Lisa Maybe it died.
Eddie Maybe it did. (*Pause*) I'm glad she never knew. (*Pause*) She had a very sweet voice. I used to play my trumpet and she'd sing sentimental old numbers. Give a little concert. Singalongs. Except everyone would gradually stop singing and listen to Millie. She'd look away into the distance and fold her rough little hands together in her lap and she'd sing. True and pure and honest. Magic.

Lisa is deep in thought

What's up?
Lisa I'm trying to think of an angle.
Eddie Angle! (*Crossly*) Are you in the right job?

Lisa starts packing up

Millie's Tale

Lisa I don't think this is a story for the *Advertiser*.
Eddie Look, imagine it's your own gran.
Lisa I don't think so. Mine was a right cow. It's a family trait.
Eddie Doesn't the *Advertiser* care when a rotten thing like this happens?
Lisa Not a lot.

Lisa moves to the hall door

Eddie (*following*) Industrial bloody waste!
Lisa (*turning back*) But the nationals might. If I sex it up.
Eddie Sex it up!
Lisa Meet me in the *Crown* — after I've made some calls.

Lisa strides out and exits

Eddie moves DS

Eddie (*addressing the audience*) The little belter! Fair enough. She was right. All the nationals picked it up. Madame Elms went around very tight-arsed for a day or two. Taken some flak maybe. Then an anonymous donor paid for the funeral which put a smile on her face — or something resembling. Then she told me to clear out poor old Millie's things. No big deal. But a few days later, I needed to have a word with Mrs Elms.

Eddie moves to the hall entrance

Mrs Elms struggles in via the hall with an old narrow mattress. She is the smart, efficient, caring owner/manager of Westways. However today she is dressed in overalls as she has been working hard to bring the home up to requirement. She has a rag doll in one pocket and a mobile phone in the other

Eddie moves to help her

Mrs Elms Where were you? Lift it, Eddie! Take your share of the weight!

Eddie Right! All right! Mrs Elms, I ...
Mrs Elms Keep it off the floor, there are bits falling out! ... Watch it!

Eddie and Mrs Elms ease the mattress DS

Eddie (*turning to the front, addressing the audience*) It was never easy to have a word with Mrs Elms.

Eddie and Mrs Elms continue trying to carry the mattress across the stage towards the kitchen

Mrs Elms We're making for the yard, Eddie!
Eddie Oh. Dumping it, right?
Mrs Elms Right. Careful!
Eddie Look, about the things we cleared out of Millie's room.
Mrs Elms Clothes have gone to Oxfam — well, a couple of things.
Eddie Yeah, I binned the others. It's not that.
Mrs Elms Would you like the rag doll?
Eddie Thanks. Listen, Mrs Elms ...
Mrs Elms There's no Will of course. Mr Jevons says since there's nothing of value ... I'll spread the trinkets around the others when I see them. But you can keep the doll. Lift the mattress! Lift the mattress!
Eddie Bugger the mattress! Just pay attention!
Mrs Elms Eddie!
Eddie You know that Lottery ticket we found in Millie's bag?
Mrs Elms Eddie! You're supposed to be helping!
Eddie I checked it out. And it's a winner.
Mrs Elms What! You do choose your moments!
Eddie And wouldn't you know. It's worth rather a lot.
Mrs Elms Really? How much? Eddie, will you take your end!
Eddie A million.

Mrs Elms drops the mattress, dumbfounded

Mrs Elms How much! A million ... ?

Millie's Tale

Eddie Quid.
Mrs Elms Good God! Are you sure? Good God! Oh how sad! Poor little Millie. And all she ever possessed was a rag doll. (*Pause*) What are you looking at me like that for? What are we supposed to do? What happens?

Eddie shrugs

I wonder if we should telephone someone? The Lottery office. I'll find the number. (*She takes out her mobile phone*)
Eddie I've found the number. (*He takes a piece of paper out of his pocket*) The National Lottery centre.
Mrs Elms You've rung?
Eddie No. I found the number. That was exciting enough.
Mrs Elms But you helped them fill in their tickets for years.
Eddie Nobody ever won anything before.

Eddie holds out the paper and Mrs Elms dials

Mrs Elms (*into phone*) Is that the Lottery centre? ... (*While she waits, she takes the rag doll out of her pocket*) Here you are, Eddie. (*Into the phone*) Is that the Lottery ... ? (*She waits*)
Eddie (*taking the doll*) Thanks, Mrs E..
Mrs Elms Ah ... Lottery centre? I think we have a winning ticket ... I ... Yes. ... (*She waits; to Eddie*) She'd have liked you to have it.
Eddie I know.

Eddie gives the ticket to Mrs Elms

Mrs Elms (*into the phone*) Hallo? I think we have a big ... A very big win. ... A huge ... A million. Yes ... A million. ... A MILLION! Oh God!

Eddie grabs the phone and speaks into it

Eddie This is the Westways Rest Home. One of our residents seems to have a winning ticket. A lot of money. It was drawn a few weeks ago. What should she do? ... Yeah, I've got it here. ... Yeah. ... Yeah. ... She sends the particulars to the Lottery centre. ... Yeah ... Yeah. ...
Mrs Elms No!
Eddie (*to Mrs Elms*) He says she's to send it to ...
Mrs Elms (*shaking Eddie*) She can't! She can't! She can't, you idiot!
Eddie (*into the phone*) She can't, you idiot. Sorry. Sorry! She can't ... No. She's dead. Yeah. I said, it's an old people's home — called Westways. And she's gone west. So what should she do?
Mrs Elms *We* do! *We* do!
Eddie What should *we* do? Do we tear it up? Or would you accept a different ticket instead? (*He takes another ticket out of his pocket*) Only I bought mine at the same time. ... Ah. ... No. I see.

Mrs Elms grabs the phone back. Eddie tears up his own ticket sadly

Mrs Elms (*into the phone*) So what will happen then? ... I see. ... Yes. ... I see. Can it? ... Does it? (*She grabs Eddie's arm*) It goes to her estate. ... (*Into the phone*) But there's no-one to inherit. There aren't any Budgens. Millie hadn't anyone. ... I see. Thank you. (*She finishes the call and turns to Eddie*) She can claim it within one hundred and eighty days!
Eddie But she's dead.
Mrs Elms Even so.
Eddie Honest to God! She had nobody and nothing. Except an old rag doll. Now she's got an old rag doll — and a million pounds.
Mrs Elms I'll ring Mr Jevons. He'll know what to do.
Eddie What about the mattress?
Mrs Elms Bugger the mattress. (*She starts towards her office*)
Eddie (*mock shocked*) Mrs Elms!
Mrs Elms Put it in the yard, Eddie.
Eddie My big mouth.
Mrs Elms Not a soul but us showed up at her funeral. Millie hasn't a relative in the world.

Millie's Tale

Mrs Elms exits into her office

Eddie (*calling after her*) Wanna bet?

Eddie drags the mattress into the kitchen. He leaves the doll off stage and enters

(*Addressing the audience*) Mr Jevons said an official of the local authority had to get a Grant of Administration. Right? So they did. And they had to try to seek out any next of kin. OK? So they did that too. They advertised in the press. Worldwide. Crazy! I could have told them. I've seen it before. They only had to broadcast that there was money on offer bigtime and all around the universe wet stones turned over and Budgens came crawling out from under. Quite usual. No exaggeration. I've seen it a million times.

Mrs Elms staggers in from the hall dressed smartly and carrying a box full of letters

Mrs Elms (*wearily*) Oh my God. But it's the law.
Eddie Mad as a box of frogs
Mrs Elms Oh Eddie! If you'd just torn up that ticket.
Eddie Surely it would have been out of order, Mrs Elms.
Mrs Elms That's never bothered you before.

Mrs Elms moves towards her office. She drops some letters and picks them up

Eddie (*to the audience*) Mrs Elms and the lawyers sifted through the Budgens as their letters poured in from all points of the compass.

The doorbell rings

Mrs Elms Oh no! No more post! No!

Mrs Elms flees into her office

Eddie Then Lisa from the *Advertiser* picked up the news. I can't think who told her.

Eddie moves US *and exits into the hall. He enters showing Lisa into the room. She comes* DS, *sits and sorts out her gear*

Lisa Thanks for ringing, Eddie. I'll make it worth your while.
Eddie Music to my ears normally. But right now it's to give Millie back a bit of dignity.
Lisa (*jeering*) Oh, come on!
Eddie You type one word about Millie I don't like and ——
Lisa And what?
Eddie I'll break your effing fingers, sunshine!
Lisa (*amused*) You silver-tongued devil, you.
Eddie (*not joking*) I could mean it.
Lisa OK. OK. OK. For heaven's sake, man! Now, colour it all in for me. Everyone always thought Millie was destitute. Without a relative or anyone close in any way. Right?
Eddie Right.
Lisa You're sure it's a big win?
Eddie Think a million.
Lisa That's a big win. And you bought a ticket the same time?
Eddie Correct.
Lisa I'm surprised you didn't think of swapping the tickets.
Eddie First thing that entered my mind. But anything to do with Millie was always straight as a die. Always will be. Besides everyone knows I always do my birthday numbers!
Lisa Absurd isn't it. Millie Budgen hadn't a relative in the world. And now they're standing ten deep.
Eddie That's the form.
Lisa So it's actually a big family.
Eddie No way. Mr Jevons and Mrs Elms have been toothcombing and they're a bunch of frauds. None of them are related to Millie. Just trying their luck.
Lisa So what happens to the money? What would Millie have liked?
Eddie I don't think that comes into it.
Lisa How long do they wait before enough is enough?
Eddie We could certainly have given Millie a fancy funeral. Black horses with plumes. And a coach with glass sides — like she was Snow White.

Millie's Tale

Lisa Overkill, Eddie. (*Seeing his face*) Sorree ...

Mrs Elms enters from the office. She is carrying a letter

Lisa turns to her, notebook ready

Lisa What a story, Mrs Elms! Flushing out the Budgens. How many letters have you had so far? Eddie says there's not one that's kosher.
Mrs Elms Eddie's wrong.
Eddie What!
Mrs Elms Mr Jevons' office did a trace on this one and I think we've struck gold.
Lisa The other way round, surely.
Mrs Elms What? Oh the money would never have been ours.
Eddie No chance.
Lisa Shame. Don't you feel wild?
Mrs Elms Life isn't like that.
Lisa So who's the lucky little Budgen?
Mrs Elms It seems to be Millie's sister.
Eddie Millie never had a sister!
Mrs Elms Mr Jevons thinks this one's a possible.
Eddie Where's she been all these years then?
Mrs Elms America.
Eddie That's not Outer Mongolia. Why didn't she show up before?
Mrs Elms We'll find out when she gets here.
Lisa She's arriving soon?
Eddie A million quid? You bet she is.
Lisa I'd like to take pictures, Mrs Elms.
Mrs Elms I don't see why not.
Lisa So, we've found one beneficiary at last!

The doorbell rings

Mrs Elms exits into the hall

Eddie (*to the audience*) But we hadn't found one beneficiary. No, we'd found two. Lucky us.

Mrs Elms shows Belle and Herbie Saunter into the room. They are Americans from New Jersey

Lisa takes a picture

Belle Well, hallo! You must be Mrs Elms. (*She holds out her hand*) Belle Saunter.
Mrs Elms (*shaking hands formally*) Mr Jevons said you'd be over.
Eddie You're Millie's sister.
Belle Her younger sister. You're ...?
Eddie Eddie.
Lisa (*breaking in*) And I'm Lisa from the *Advertiser* — the local newspaper. All the nationals ran the story. There's been a fantastic interest in you.
Belle Oh, I guess. It isn't every day somebody inherits one million pound sterling just like that.
Lisa Right out of the blue.
Eddie From a stranger — well almost.
Belle What? Oh, now this is Herbie Saunter, my husband.
Herbie Hi.
Lisa I understand you've established your bona fides with the lawyers.
Belle We have too!
Herbie (*firmly*) Next of kin.
Lisa You will let me take pictures, won't you, Belle? Nice to have good news to publish.
Belle You're so right. I hope my hair's not too mussed. But I thought we'd make our visit to the home right away.
Herbie I told Belle it wasn't necessary.
Eddie That's right. Millie didn't have any belongings.
Mrs Elms Eddie. Give it a rest.
Belle It was Mr Jevons suggested it. Said I might like to see where my sister spent her last days. We lost touch, you know.
Eddie For forty years, wasn't it?
Herbie Who is this guy?!
Mrs Elms A carer here at Westways.
Eddie A very close friend of Millie's.

Millie's Tale 13

Herbie Oh I get it.
Belle Herbie!
Herbie We can't help it if the old girl didn't leave him anything!
Mrs Elms She didn't leave anybody anything. There *was* nothing. The Lottery prize came up after she was dead.
Herbie We know that!
Lisa Picture please!

Herbie and Belle lean together and smile

Lisa takes a photo

Great! Great stuff! So, you lost touch with your sister when you went to the States?
Belle Millie and I were on our uppers at the time. Meeting Herbie was a godsend. He was so handsome. (*To Herbie*) Well, you were! Everybody fancied you. (*Giggling*) But I landed him. It was a chance for a new life.
Eddie But didn't you hear Millie was in trouble?
Herbie There was nothing Belle could do.
Belle Millie didn't say anything. We were at the very point of leaving when she began to show. (*She pats her stomach*)
Herbie We had our own problems. I was just starting up ——
Belle Herbie's in electronics.
Herbie —— my own business. Made the contacts I needed in the UK. And all set to build it up.
Belle And we did. Worked all hours God gave. Thirty years of slog. This is the first overseas vacation we've had. We intend to do every sight in town, don't we, Herb?
Herbie Yeah. Yeah.
Lisa You'll be going on a shopping spree?
Belle You betcha! (*Laughing excitedly*) I need clothes! Clothes!
Eddie So you left Millie to cope on her own.
Belle Well, *she* got herself pregnant on her own, didn't she?
Lisa Who was the father?
Belle One of those horny guys on the building site, Herbie figured.
Herbie I figured.

Belle Millie said they were real strong-looking.
Herbie Too easy for her own good.
Belle (*reproaching*) Oh, Herbie! But it's true. She could be — over-affectionate.
Eddie Too trusting, maybe.
Herbie (*looking at Eddie*) You found that, did you?
Lisa What about a picture with Mrs Elms, now?
Belle Sure, dear. Herbie!
Herbie For God's sake. How many?
Lisa And maybe that old rag doll.
Mrs Elms Ah ... Do you mind, Eddie?

Eddie hesitates then exits into the kitchen

Lisa groups the Saunters and Mrs Elms, and takes a picture

Awkward pause

Herbie Well, Belle couldn't do anything. Next thing we heard Millie had been committed and ...
Mrs Elms Millie was never committed.
Herbie Well, whatever you call it over here.
Lisa We call it sectioned.
Mrs Elms She was never sectioned! She was never sectioned.
Herbie OK. OK. She was put in a mental institution. Am I right?
Mrs Elms And she got better.
Herbie If she got so better what was she doing here?
Mrs Elms This is simply an old peoples' home. It was decided she'd be best in a controlled situation where she could be safe and cared for yet useful and occupied. It gave a bit of dignity to her life. To a certain extent earning her keep.
Herbie (*to Belle*) You get it, honey ... Earning her keep.
Mrs Elms To a certain extent.
Herbie I'll bet.

Mrs Elms is about to retort but stops short as ——

Eddie enters with the doll

Eddie Here.

Lisa takes it and gives it to Belle

Lisa Great! Caption ... Millie Budgen's worldly goods — one million pounds and an old rag doll — inherited by her sister Belle. (*She takes a photo*)
Mrs Elms No. The doll belongs to Eddie. I gave it to him.
Herbie If you don't mind ... It's ours.
Mrs Elms Sorry. I suppose so.
Lisa You have children? Grandchildren?
Herbie Oh keep it. It's no big deal.
Belle (*nursing the doll*) I'd like it, Herbie ...
Herbie Oh God, none of that. We do not have children. Never wanted them. OK, Belle?
Belle OK, Herbie.

Belle holds out the doll. Mrs Elms takes it and gives it back to Eddie

Herbie Kids were not our scene.
Lisa So, after your shopping spree, what will you do with the bulk of the money?
Herbie I have plans.
Belle Oh we'll get a fancy condo in Florida and maybe a yacht! But then we'd need a permanent crew — Herbie can't sail a rubber duck! Then change the car. Oh yes! I know ...
Herbie Hold it, kid.
Eddie I think this calls for champagne. (*He makes for the kitchen*)
Mrs Elms What?

Lisa and Mrs Elms stare at Eddie

Eddie exits. Mrs Elms out hurries after him

Lisa Maybe a picture in Millie's old room, eh?

Belle Her room?
Lisa The old folk are not here.
Belle I did wonder ...
Lisa Building works going on.
Herbie We don't need to see the room.
Lisa What about a picture of you looking through a stonemason's catalogue? Looking for a suitable headstone, you know.
Herbie A headstone?
Lisa For Millie. (*She rummages in her bag*) I just happen to have one.
Belle A headstone.
Herbie A catalogue, dumbbell.
Lisa You sit together looking serious and studying it and ——
Herbie I don't think we'll be buying a headstone.
Lisa No? Well!
Belle Of course we will, Herbie. It's called for, don't you see?
Herbie No, I don't.
Lisa (*making a note*) The Saunters do not plan to set a memorial over Millie Budgen's unmarked grave.
Herbie Give me that catalogue! Belle, choose what you think Millie would enjoy on top of her.

Herbie and Belle pose with the catalogue

Lisa takes a photo

Belle studies an item, frowning

Belle What's a "catafalque", Herbie?
Herbie Where they bury cats — how do I know?
Lisa By the way, you do know that Westways is having a rough passage right now. Confidentially, a donation to its refurbishment would be very popular.
Belle That would be good. Me handing a cheque to Mrs Elms for ... You decide, Herbie.
Herbie Five hundred dollars.

Pause

Millie's Tale   17

Belle Lisa, could you give us a moment alone, please?
Lisa Sure. Five hundred dollars. Wicked.

Lisa exits into the kitchen

Belle What sort of cheapskate are you? (*She's disgusted*)
Herbie Tough. It's my money.
Belle Our money, Herbie. What's mine is yours and yours is mine. We always agreed.
Herbie Mine was yours, right enough.
Belle Come again? Who spent all the hours God gave on her knees scrubbing the floor of the apartment, the little shop, the house, the emporium! Me me me!
Herbie Scrubbing the floor?
Belle Metaphorically! Who stacked shelves, checked bills, balanced books, hired staff, fired staff. Me me me! Who helped you set up the biggest and best electronics business in town? Me me me! Five hundred dollars. I could die! It's our place to make gestures, Herbie. (*Scornfully*) Five hundred dollars! Honest to God!
Herbie Belle! Can it! Listen up. Have you cast your eye on the new electronics store on tenth street? Prime spot on the corner. Did you see the name over that store? No. You haven't tittuped down town in months. It's just the biggest chain in the States. There are goodies in that store I hadn't even heard of. OK, so I've not kept up. The gear changes so fast ... Fact is I need to restock like crazy to get up to speed. This legacy is some timely lifebelt, kid. And you want to fling it around like a drunken sailor. It could get us back on track. I know our business better than those wet-eared kids they've let loose in their store. I know our customers. I'm the store they trust. But, jeez, I need money, Belle.
Belle Herbie, you never said. It's really that bad?
Herbie I was waiting for the right moment to tell you. And I'm telling you — there never is the right moment!
Belle (*quietly*) You should have said. (*Pause*) You need all of it?
Herbie (*angrily*) There you go! (*Pause*) I guess you can have a gown.

Belle Thanks, doll. Don't worry — we'll give them a fight! We've done it once and we'll do it again! And you're right — five hundred dollars will do for this dump.
Herbie Didn't your sister supply cheap labour all those years?
Belle Yeah! We don't owe them anything.

Eddie enters from the kitchen carrying a champagne bottle. Lisa follows

Eddie Party-time!

Eddie shakes the bottle and makes to open it. The Saunters and Lisa duck out of range. But it's a conjurer's trick bottle and as Eddie shouts "bang!" he brings a bunch of feathers out of the neck. Eddie presents them to Belle

Herbie (*irritated*) What sort of gag is that!?
Eddie You didn't think we kept champers on the premises, did you? ... One of my props from the old days.

Mrs Elms appears at the hall entrance

Mrs Elms There's a mug of tea in the dining-room for everybody.
Belle Oh. Oh thanks.

Lisa makes to take a picture

Belle No more pictures until I get to a beauty parlour!
Eddie You need a perm? Wet your finger and stick it in the light socket.
Mrs Elms That's not funny, Eddie.
Eddie The old girls think it's hilarious.

Mrs Elms and Belle exit into the hall

Lisa Eddie was in show business. Before he decided to come here.
Herbie (*to Eddie*) You made the right choice, feller.

Millie's Tale

Lisa exits into the hall and Herbie follows

Eddie comes DS

Eddie (*addressing audience*) They were everything I don't like in people. Difficult to see any part of our Millie in that Belle. Oh, they pranced around in the limelight. Promised two thousand dollars to Westways in the end. Prized out of them by Lisa. I was beginning to appreciate her special talent. None of us felt joy at those Saunters scooping up the Lottery. Lisa less than any of us. She started doing some digging in archives, checking some dates, making calls to old friends in the north, jiggled around on the Internet. The Saunters meantime enjoyed their moment of fame. Herbie did some business deals. Then came the time when they were set to go home to New Jersey with their sack of gold. I was surprised when Lisa announced she needed one final picture here at the home. Mrs Elms and I got out our sickbags. But Lisa was adamant. So the Saunters showed up, ready for a big sentimental photoshoot. But Lisa hadn't arrived yet. Unlike Lisa.

Mrs Elms enters showing in Belle and Herbie from the hall. Belle wears a showercoat which she removes. Herbie gives an umbrella to Mrs Elms and shakes the rain from his hat

Herbie (*consulting his watch*) We can give you exactly thirty minutes.
Mrs Elms I'll give Lisa a ring. There must be a good reason.

Mrs Elms exits into the hall

Eddie (*to the audience*) There was. The good reason arrived with Lisa.

Lisa enters, guiding in Sandra. Sandra is attractive and around forty. She has an Australian accent. She looks about the room. Mrs Elms follows slowly, staring at Sandra

Pause

Lisa This is Sandra Budgen. Millie's daughter.

Big reaction

There's no question about it. We have a copy of her birth certificate — at long last.

Sandra takes the document from her bag and holds it out to Mrs Elms and Eddie

Belle sits down, stunned

Mrs Elms (*taking Sandra's hand*) I'm Patricia Elms. And I'm ... I'm speechless! Eddie!

Eddie is gazing at Sandra

Eddie and your mother were very good friends
Eddie (*gently*) Millie's daughter. (*He moves to Sandra*) And the first thing you get is a shower of rain.
Sandra I enjoyed it.

Eddie helps her off with her coat

Sandra sits to put the document back in her bag. She watches and listens to everyone

Herbie (*confused*) I don't get it.
Eddie Funny you should say that.
Belle (*softly*) Sandra.
Mrs Elms (*to Lisa*) How in the world did you find her?
Lisa Journalists have noses — a sixth sense — good memories ...
Eddie Contacts.
Lisa You got it. The baby having disappeared ...

Mrs Elms We just couldn't get any more news. They implied she'd been adopted.
Lisa I could find no record of the child being adopted. If I had, that would have been the end of it. It was a mystery. Where do flies go in the winter? Where do babies go when they're not with their mothers or fathers or adopted or fostered or in a children's home? There was just this one thought. And it nagged and nagged. Could she have been migrated? Sent out of the country.
Eddie Millie would never have agreed to that.
Mrs Elms Millie was never asked. I'd swear to it.
Lisa I hunted around really hard and began to suspect it more and more. I got help. I found people who knew all about this. We began to look closer at those migrant children. The orphans — so-called — sent overseas to the Commonwealth.
Mrs Elms But not at that time surely! I know in the twenties and thirties ...
Lisa There were ten thousand children sent *after* World War II ... Don't you understand? The last ones only went in nineteen sixty-seven!
Mrs Elms I can't believe it.
Lisa Well, I found out. Ten thousand little kids shipped off into the unknown. Horrendous.
Mrs Elms And Millie's child was one of them?
Lisa Sandra was one of them.
Mrs Elms Oh my God! But she must have been just tiny.
Sandra A good way to get rid of the riff-raff.
Belle Don't say that.
Sandra But it's true.

A pause

Lisa takes Sandra's hand and guides her nearer the Saunters. Belle rises

Lisa This is Belle ... Your aunt — and her husband. Belle, this is your niece — Sandra. You did know Millie christened her Sandra?

Belle nods. Long pause. Lisa moves away. Sandra stares at Belle

Sandra (*at last; quietly bitter*) Why did you do it? How could you do it?

Belle looks at Herbie. He doesn't respond. An awkward pause

Mrs Elms (*to Lisa*) But how did you make contact?
Lisa I put all the details on the Internet.
Eddie A real use for it at last.
Mrs Elms We could never find out anything about Sandra.
Sandra (*angrily*) Because I was twelve thousand miles away, wasn't I! And you weren't meant to! We were to have no baggage — no past. No families were to follow us out. We were to be instant Australians!
Lisa So logical!
Sandra Every toy, every bit of clothing from home was taken away — for good. We had come up overnight with the mushrooms!
Lisa A bit of human engineering ...
Sandra We were biddable, malleable, trainable. To be broken in! Well nobody comes up with the mushrooms! We all come from somewhere — whatever it's like.
Lisa It was to solve a problem here and fill a need there.
Sandra I'd always been in a children's home. Never been anywhere else that I knew of. I might not have been loved ... I didn't know what that was anyway. At least I wasn't despised, illtreated. I was settled in a routine with all the other children. Then there came a day ... I remember it — so well. Can never forget. The day they came in and said "Who wants to go to Australia?" And I put up my hand with the others and shouted with them "Me! Me!" I thought it was a day's outing. I was four years old. Next thing I was on a huge ship and seasick and crying and messing myself. I didn't know what was happening to me. Nobody said. Nobody explained. Then I was in just another children's home. But I knew no-one and it was terribly hot and miles and miles from anywhere, just scrub and bushland. And there were Australian children who teased me because I was English trash. And I was

Millie's Tale

frightened of the snakes and spiders. And I wet the bed and they made me stand with my wet sheet over my head. I was four years old. And everything and everybody was strange. And nobody, nobody cared!
Belle (*quietly*) I thought you'd got adopted.
Sandra Why didn't *you* adopt me! They said my mother was dead. That I had no relatives. They said I'd go to a farm and have an auntie and uncle. That we'd all be adopted. Supposed to be fostered out. But it wasn't like that at all. It was lies! We were worth more to them as orphans in the homes, you see. There were subsidies paid for us. It's always down to money, you know! Oh I went to a farm later on. I was told to milk the cows but I didn't know how and they laughed at me and I started to wet the bed again and I got thrashed for it! (*Emotion is overcoming her*) And there was no-one to tell out there in the bush, thousands of miles from anywhere! I didn't know where I was or who I was! And I knew no-one would ever, ever come! (*She weeps*)

Eddie goes to Sandra

I'm sorry. I'm sorry.
Belle I didn't know anything about that!
Eddie You knew about Millie!
Herbie Stop sniping at Belle. She had a right to a life of her own.
Sandra (*rounding on Herbie*) Why didn't you help my mother? What happened? Was my mother a fool?

Lisa, Eddie and Mrs Elms draw Sandra aside to calm her

Mrs Elms (*gently*) Listen, Sandra, when Millie gave birth to you, she had a really rough time. Fifty-two hours in labour, apparently.
Eddie She told me it broke all the veins in her eyes.
Mrs Elms And her mind went, Sandra. She had to be cared for — in an institution. For a while.
Belle But we'd gone to the States by then.
Eddie (*to Belle*) But you knew!
Belle Well — a friend sent letters ... But I swear I never knew about Sandra being sent abroad.

Herbie You don't have to defend yourself, Belle. What was your government doing? They're the ones who sent the child.
Lisa No. It was the private charities and religious agencies who were sending them out. They had their orphanages here teeming with abandoned children and there was Australia with vast empty spaces and a great climate and desperate for immigrants.
Sandra But nobody ever explained to us children! We thought we'd done something awful, something unforgivable.
Lisa I guess it was OK for some kids. You can see the reasoning. But it was dangerous. And cruel.
Sandra To take away our identity — completely. To tell us we had no-one who cared about us. To tell our relatives we'd been adopted! To lie!
Lisa When it went wrong it went very, very wrong. There were some terribly damaged children.
Herbie (*exasperated*) OK. Can we give this a rest now!
Belle Herbie!
Herbie Well, in spite of it, Sandra doesn't look so bad to me!

Outraged, Mrs Elms, Lisa and Eddie press in on Herbie overlapping each other

Mrs Elms It's to her credit she made a life!
Eddie You've got a nerve!
Lisa If you had a bit of imagination!
Eddie You left, knowing Millie couldn't cope!
Mrs Elms And you don't care what happened to her child!

Herbie It's the past! She's OK, isn't she? She's alive! She's healthy! She's just won a pot of dough for sweet all. I earned every cent I got the hard way!
Belle (*backing Herbie*) Other people have problems!
Herbie Don't lay this on me! It's not my beeswax!
Sandra (*violently*) You bloody mongrel!

Sandra attacks Herbie. Belle steps between them forcefully

Belle You stop that! That's enough now!

Millie's Tale

Sandra backs off and joins the others. She sits

Sandra (*wryly*) Is this "family"?
Mrs Elms (*gently*) Sometimes.

Eddie glares at Herbie and moves to Sandra's side

Eddie So, what happened, Sandra?
Sandra I was sent out as a domestic. I had to learn everything as I went along. The farmer's wife said if I tore the pancakes again she'd hold my hand on the griddle. But I'd never made a pancake in my life. I ran away but there was nowhere to go and they caught me easily. I was sent to another farm where the woman was nice. But the farmer tried to get at me at night. I was sent back to the children's home eventually. But they never believed anything I said. When I was sixteen I went to work in a hotel. I got paid properly at last. And I was free. And then I met a good man. A really good man. And I married him.
Belle A happy ending. Thank God.
Eddie Pity Millie's happy ending came too late.
Sandra I had no idea she was still alive. I always dreamed of tracing my mother. But they said there were no records. It was a lie. Just another lie. When I grew up I wondered if she was really dead. I had this strange feeling. If she was alive then surely she would remember me. No mother can forget a child of her womb, surely. Then I thought if she'd let me go like that, then I didn't want to know her anyway.
Mrs Elms She never knew, I promise you. She was never capable of looking after you but she believed you were being well cared for. We all did.

Eddie takes the doll from his pocket

Eddie (*to Sandra*) See this? She loved this old rag doll as if it was you. Said she'd give it to you one day to play with.

Sandra touches the doll

Mrs Elms Not realizing the years had passed. Not understanding. She was a sweet woman, your mother. She latched on to Eddie when she came here. He was her anchor. He made her laugh. They were a double act.
Eddie We were a double act.
Mrs Elms There's a sort of personality that can weave a thread of good cheer through life. I had it here in Westways because of Eddie and Millie. There was fun around the place — because of them.
Eddie You do your best, Mrs E.
Mrs Elms That'll do! What I'm saying is, Sandra, that your mother gave us something invaluable. And I'm grateful. And I want you to know that about her. And she never stopped loving you. You and that doll were one in her mind.
Eddie It's yours now, Sandra. (*He offers the doll*)
Sandra (*pushing it away gently*) I wish so much I'd found her in time. She could have told me who I am. You need to know who you are. A vacuum is unbearable.
Mrs Elms It was wicked not to let her see her records.
Lisa They had this notion — that it was best the children have no more contact with their homeland. Best that they grow up and populate the country with sound white British stock.
Belle Real sad you didn't come home sooner.
Sandra (*sharply*) I applied for a British passport. And they told me I didn't exist!
Belle You were very unlucky.
Sandra There were others, I can tell you. Far and away unluckier than me. Broken lives. (*Pause. She glances around*) To think this might have been my country. Where I might have grown up. I never expected to come here.
Belle Well, nor did I!

A pause. Mrs Elms looks round at the group

Mrs Elms Nobody ever came to see Millie when she was alive.
Sandra (*to Herbie*) They turned up soon enough at the smell of money.

Herbie So did you.
Belle Oh, Herbie, stop it. I always wanted to contact Millie, but you wouldn't let me. That so?
Herbie No point stirring up old emotions. That's how it was.
Belle You didn't want to get lumbered. That's how it was!
Herbie (*pointing at Sandra*) Fact remains, she'll do very nicely now, thank you! Yeah. Whereas ... Whereas ... (*He slumps, defeated*) Oh heck.
Belle (*going to Herbie*) Oh hon, I know how you feel.
Eddie (*with irony*) I think I do too.
Herbie (*quietly*) No way you do. (*Turning on Sandra*) And since we're so hot on family, how's about sharing the money with your aunt!?
Sandra I didn't come over because of the money.
Herbie Well we did! Let's have a tad honesty around here.
Sandra I came to find out the truth about my mother. And about myself.
Herbie And for the money.
Belle Sandra, I'm glad things worked out for you in the end. I truly regret not helping Millie when I might have. But we didn't have things easy in the beginning, Herbie and me. (*She moves to Sandra*) And truth to tell, we're in a spot again. (*She puts her hand on Sandra's arm*) It's a whole load of money, Sandra.
Eddie I don't believe it!
Mrs Elms Sandra, it's *your* inheritance.
Lisa Right! You can spend the rest of your life at ease, Sandra. You certainly deserve it!
Belle Blood is thicker than water, Sandra.
Herbie Oh shut your face, Belle. What's the use?
Sandra Lisa told me a lot about the setup here. And I've done some thinking. And I'll tell you now. I shall give half the money to Westways.
Mrs Elms Oh my God! Oh my God! No, Sandra, you can't.
Sandra I can do anything in the world I like now, actually. Half to Westways. Meet all those bloody regulations. Build on to the place. Put in a swimming-pool. Do what you like. I'll set up a Trust.

Mrs Elms Oh my God! (*She starts to cry*)
Eddie (*astonished*) Mrs E.!
Mrs Elms (*drying up at once*) That will be absolutely splendid. I won't waste a penny. I never do.
Eddie She never does.
Sandra And Eddie. How does a hundred thousand sound?
Eddie I don't need that. If Westways is set fair, then I'm set fair. Right, Mrs E.?
Mrs Elms I knew there was a catch.
Sandra No, Eddie, it's for you. You'll need a pension sometime. Have some fun. Come over and visit me occasionally.
Eddie You mean it?
Sandra You started all this, didn't you? Caring for my mother.
Eddie You're very like her when you smile. You're very much her little girl.
Belle Have you children, Sandra?
Sandra I have two boys.
Belle Oh. Hear that, Herbie? I have two great-nephews.
Herbie Yeah.
Sandra They were my saving. (*Pause*) I couldn't cuddle them at first. Didn't know how. I'd never been cuddled. By anyone. My husband taught me tenderness. He's six feet five of barn door. But he taught me tenderness. Time passes. The boys are grown up now. It was one of them ... Roy ... who picked up the details that Lisa put on the Net ... It was an incredible moment. I couldn't stop shaking.
Eddie What do they do — the boys?
Sandra They work with us. On the cattle station. In Queensland. I married a farmer.
Eddie Too much to hope they'd be in showbusiness.
Sandra Too much. But they like to fly down to Sydney to see the shows.
Eddie That costs!
Sandra We have a plane.
Mrs Elms A cattle station.
Sandra Fifty thousand acres.
Belle A large house, I'll bet.

Sandra Big enough. Sixty kilometres from the front gate. I told you I didn't come for the money. So. If you can use the rest — Auntie Belle?

Sandra and Belle slowly turn and regard one another. Belle grasps at Herbie

Belle Let's see — that's around five hundred thousand dollars.
Eddie Sandra!
Sandra It's not because I like them, Eddie. But they're part of me. I've longed all my life to belong to someone — a family. It doesn't matter what sort of people — that's part of it all. Belle has the answers to all the questions, the background — the way-back background. She'll tell me. She'll write it all down. My kith and kin.
Belle Of course, dear.
Eddie But Sandra ...
Sandra Eddie, they're no spring chickens and the USA is no place to be a failure.
Herbie Nowhere is a place to be a failure, baby.
Belle Five hundred grand. Can we manage with that, Herbie?
Herbie Belle! A month ago we had none of it! I'll manage!
Belle (*slipping her arm though Herbie's, devotedly*) He's a tiger!

Herbie pats Belle's hand. Then he moves to face Sandra. Now we see there is perhaps a likeness between Herbie and Sandra

Herbie That's generous, kid.
Eddie She's just like her mother. Looks like her too.

Belle moves between Herbie and Sandra looking from one to the other. Her hand goes to her mouth as a thought crosses her mind. Eddie sees this and holds out the doll to Sandra

Eddie This is yours, Sandra. Keep it safe. Your mother loved it for a lifetime.
Sandra (*offering doll to Belle*) You have the doll. I have real children.

Belle takes the doll and holds it

Herbie We need to be off. Belle! (*He gives Belle her coat and crosses to hall entrance where he turns. To all*) Be seeing you. Maybe.

Herbie exits in to the hall

Belle starts for the hall. She turns back, holding the doll to her body. She gives a long, puzzled, almost tender look at Sandra. Then follows Herbie out quickly

Pause

Sandra Mrs Elms, is there a photograph of my mother?
Mrs Elms I think there's a group somewhere ... And there was one in her room — that Eddie took of her.
Eddie I've got it here.

He takes the photo from his breast pocket and gives it to Sandra. Sandra looks at it, intently

Pause

Lisa aims the camera to Sandra

Lisa May I?
Sandra (*nods; turning to Mrs Elms*) Could I have a few moments in my mother's old room, please?
Mrs Elms (*nodding*) Come on!

Sandra looks back with a smile at Eddie. Lisa takes another picture. Sandra gives the photo back to Eddie

   Sandra and Mrs Elms exit into the hall

Lisa (*thoughtfully*) Do you think ...? Is it possible? Herbie ...?

Eddie Who knows?
Lisa (*gathering her gear*) I've got to get this story in, Eddie. See you later?
Eddie (*nodding*) Crown.

Lisa exits into hall

Eddie moves DS *to address audience*

Who knows? It doesn't matter now. What matters is — we've got Millie's girl. Safe and sound. And I intend to do everything to make it up to her. (*He regards the photo, fondly*) For Millie's sake. (*Looking heavenwards*) What do you think, Millie? In the end, you were the one to save Westways. Well done, old sausage. Yes, in the end, it was all up to you. Funny that. It's amazing how useful some of it can be — this "industrial waste" ... (*Pause*) Not a dry seat in the house, Millie.

The Lights slowly fade to Black-out

CURTAIN

FURNITURE AND PROPERTY LIST

On stage: Three chairs
Divan seat

Off stage: Old narrow mattress (**Mrs Elms**)
Box full of letters (**Mrs Elms**)
Letter (**Mrs Elms**)
Trick champagne bottle (see author's note) (**Eddie**)
Umbrella (**Herbie**)

Personal: **Eddie**: screwdriver, letter, piece of paper, 2 Lottery tickets, photograph
Lisa: bag containing tiny recorder, notebook and pen, camera, headstone catalogue
Mrs Elms: rag doll, mobile phone
Sandra: handbag containing a birth certificate

LIGHTING PLOT

Practical fittings required: nil
1 interior same throughout

To open: General interior lighting

Cue 1:   **Eddie**: "Not a dry seat in the house, Millie."   (Page 31)
         Slow fade to Black-out

EFFECTS PLOT

Cue 1 **Eddie**: "Anyway, this reporter showed up." (Page 2)
Doorbell ring

Cue 2 **Eddie**: "... from all points of the compass." (Page 9)
Doorbell ring

Cue 3 **Lisa**: "...found one beneficiary at last!" (Page 11)
Doorbell ring